A Father's Book
of Prayers

Regina Press
New York

First published in Great Britain in 1994 by
KEVIN MAYHEW LTD
Rattlesden
Bury St Edmunds
Suffolk IP30 OSZ

© 1994 Kevin Mayhew Limited

*Dedicated to the memory of our dear friend,
Harry Costello. We will miss you, and always treasure
the memories of our times together.*

GEORGE AND ROBERT

ISBN 088271 495 3

1996 The Regina Press

Printed in Belgium

CONTENTS

	Page
As a father	10
Be still	9
Be at Peace	31
Children, obey your parents	22
Don't Quit	12
Everything is Possible	22
Father of the Prodigal	14
Genesis	6
God Has Not Promised	9
God Makes the Difference	5
If I Could	20
I love you	31
Jesus said	25
Joseph's Meditation	27
Learning to Live	16
Life's Lessons	28
Lord, you have given	8
Love is patient	18
Which of you fathers	24
You did not receive	11

GOD MAKES THE DIFFERENCE

In all of our days,
in so many wonderful,
beautiful ways,
the blessings he sends
from his own loving hand,
are better than anything
we could have planned.

His love for his children
is daily expressed;
like a father he gives
nothing less than his best.

His gifts and his goodness
fill life to the brim,
with a joy that could only
be fashioned by him.

GENESIS

God, we call you 'Father,'
and we think it says
something about you.
Does is not also say
something about fatherhood?
You are the God who lets be:
'Let there be light',
'Let there be land',
'Let there be stars'.
Is that what fatherhood is?
Not domination, but partnership,
not imposition, but influence,
not coercion but involvement.

That's risky:
it can lead to pain.
It *did* lead to pain:
a grieving Father,
a desolate Son,
yet still united
by a broken Spirit.
And in all of that,
through all of that,
the promise of life abundant.

God, if that's what it takes
to be a father,
if that's what it takes
to offer life to another,
give me grace to be a father.
Give me grace to let be.

MICHAEL FORSTER

Lord, you have given
so much to me.
Give one thing more:
a grateful heart.

GOD HAS NOT PROMISED

God has not promised
sun without rain,
joy without sorrow,
peace without pain.
But God has promised
strength for the day,
rest for the labour,
light for the way,
grace for the trials,
help from above,
unfailing sympathy,
undying love.

Be still, and know
that I am God.

PSALM 46:10

As a father has compassion on his children, so the Lord has compassion on those who fear him.

PSALM 103:13

You did not receive a spirit that makes you a slave again to fear, but you received the Spirit of sonship. And by him we cry, 'Abba, Father.'

ROMANS 8:15

Don't Quit

When things go wrong
as they sometimes will;
when the road you are trudging
seems all uphill;
when funds are low and debts are high
and you want to smile
but you have to sigh;
when care is pressing you down a bit,
rest, if you must,
but don't you quit.

Life is strange
with its twists and turns,
as every one of us sometimes learns,
and many a failure turns about
when they might have won,
had they stuck it out.

Don't give up
though the pace seems slow.
You may succeed with another blow.
Success is failure turned inside out,
the silver tint of the cloud of doubt,

and you never can tell
how close you are;
it may be near when is seems so far.

So stick to the fight
when you're hardest hit.
It's when things seem worst
you must not quit.

13

Father of the Prodigal

I let you go away,
knowing you were foolish.
What else should I have done?
Should I have caged you,
refused your rightful request,
denied your freedom,
your dignity,
your responsibility?

14

I let you go away.
I didn't want to.
I wanted to hold you,
protect you,
keep you a child.
Perhaps you'll learn,
perhaps you'll regret,
perhaps you'll come home.
But you've got to do it.
Yourself.
Of your own volition.
Because you're free,
and because you're responsible.
Meanwhile, I wait, and I watch.
That's hard:
harder than clinging,
and harder than forsaking.

I hope you'll come.
I'm longing to welcome you:
no recriminations, no reproof,
no 'I told you so' . . .
Just love.

MICHAEL FORSTER
BASED ON LUKE 15:11-24

LEARNING TO LIVE

If a child lives with criticism
he learns to condemn.
If a child lives with hostility
he learns to fight.
If a child lives with ridicule
he learns to be shy.
If a child lives with shame
he learns to feel guilty.
If a child lives with tolerance
he learns to be patient.

If a child lives with encouragement
he learns confidence.
If a child lives with praise
he learns to appreciate.
If a child lives with fairness
he learns justice.
If a child lives with security
he learns to have faith.
If a child lives with approval
he learns to like himself.
If a child lives with acceptance
and friendship
he learns to find love in the world.

Love is patient and kind;
it is not jealous or conceited or proud;
Love is not ill-mannered
or selfish or irritable;
Love does not keep a record of wrongs;

Love is not happy with evil
but is happy with the truth.
Love never gives up;
and its faith, hope and patience
never fail.

I Corinthians 13:4-7

If I Could

If I could, I would teach
each child to be positive,
to smile, to love and be loved.

I would teach each child to take time
to observe some miracle of nature –
the song of a bird,
the beauty of a snowflake,
the orange glow of a winter sunset.

I would teach each child to feel warmly
about those for whom the task of learning
does not come easily.

I would teach each one to be kind
to all living creatures
and to crowd out of their lives
feelings of guilt, misunderstanding
and lack of compassion.

I would teach each child that it is alright
to show their feelings by laughing,
crying, or touching someone they care about.

Everyday I would have a child feel special
and through my actions,
each one would know how much
I really care.

EVERYTHING IS POSSIBLE

This is impossible
for a human being,
but for God
everything is possible.

MATTHEW 19:26

Children, obey your parents in the Lord, for
this is right. 'Honour your father and
mother' – which is the first commandment
with a promise – 'that it may go well with
you and that you may enjoy long life on the
earth.' Fathers, do not exasperate your
children; instead, bring them up in the
training and instruction of the Lord.

EPHESIANS 6:1-4

23

Which of you fathers, if your son asks for a fish, will give him a snake instead? Or if he asks for an egg, will give him a scorpion? If you then, though you are evil, know how to give good gifts to your children, how much more will your Father in heaven give the Holy Spirit to those who ask him!

Luke 11:11-13

Jesus said, 'Do not hold on to me, for I have not yet returned to the Father. Go instead to my brothers and tell them, "I am returning to my Father and your Father, to my God and your God."'

JOHN 20:17

Joseph's Meditation

What are you to me,
and I to you?
Can you call me 'father'?
May I call you 'son'?
Is fatherhood a matter of biology?
Or sonship about genetics?
If it is,
what can we be to each other?

Or is it more a question
of relating,
rather than relatedness?
We can love each other,
teach each other,
share with each other,
laugh and cry with each other.
That's what it's about:
mutuality.
I can only be 'father',
in relation to you as 'son'.
We need each other.

MICHAEL FORSTER

LIFE'S LESSONS

After a while
you learn the difference
between holding a hand
and chaining a soul.
You learn that love isn't leaning,
but lending support.
You begin to accept your defeats
with the grace of an adult,
not the grief of a child.

You decide to build
your roads on today,
for tomorrow's ground
is too uncertain.
You help someone plant a garden
instead of waiting
for someone to bring you flowers.
You learn that God has given you
the strength to endure,
and that you really do have worth.

Be at Peace

Do not look forward
to what might happen tomorrow;
the same everlasting Father
who cares for you today
will take care of you
tomorrow and every day.
Be at peace, then, and put aside
all anxious thoughts and imaginings.

Francis de Sales

I love you
with an everlasting love.

Jeremiah 31:3

ACKNOWLEDGEMENTS

The publishers wish to express their gratitude to Fine Art Photographic Library, London and the Galleries listed below for permission to reproduce the pictures in this publication:

Front cover A CORNFIELD by George Turner (1843-1910).
Fine Art of Oakham.

Page 4 THE VILLAGE STREET, EYNSFORD, KENT
by John William Buxton Knight (1843-1908). Haynes Fine Art, Broadway.

Page 7 OVER THE GATE by Juan Antonio Benliure (1855-1937).

Page 8 DERNIERS RAYONS by Georges Phillbert Charles Maroniez (1865-1933).
Eaton Gallery, London SW1.

Pages 10 & 11 THE VILLAGE CRICKET MATCH by Basil Holmes (fl.1844-1850).
Beaton Brown Paintings, London SW1.

Page 13 RABBITS IN AUTUMN COLOURS by Henry Carter (fl.1860-1894).
Julian Simon Gallery, London SW3.

Page 14 A SWEDISH LANDSCAPE WITH POPPIES by Johan Erik Ericson (1849-1925).
Omell Galleries, London SW1.

Page 17 THE CONISTON VALLEY, THE LAKE DISTRICT
by William Lakin Turner (1867-1936). Colmore Galleries, Henley-in-Arden.

Pages 18 & 19 CANTERBURY CATHEDRAL FROM THE STOUR
by Dan Sherrin (fl.1895-1915).

Page 20 WINTER ALERT by Moritz Muller (1841-1899).

Page 23 OUTSIDE THE SHIP'S INN (detail) by Henry Sykes (1855-1921).
St Peter's Fine Art.

Pages 24 & 25 THE BEACH AT ST. IVES by William H. Borrow (fl.1865).
Hampshire Gallery.

Page 26 FISHING FROM A PUNT by A.W. Redgate (fl.1886-1901).

Page 29 A VIEW IN THE ALPS (detail) by Sigvard Marius Hansen (b.1859).
Burlington Gallery, London W1.

Page 30 THE LAKE IN THE WOODS by P.M. Monsted (1859-1941).
Burlington Gallery, London W1.